Little Pebble™

Our Families

T0052231

Sisters Are Part of a Family

by Lucia Raatma

CAPSTONE PRESS
a capstone imprint

Little Pebble is published by Capstone Press,
1710 Roe Crest Drive, North Mankato, Minnesota 56003
www.mycapstone.com

Copyright © 2018 by Capstone Press, a Capstone imprint. All rights reserved.
No part of this publication may be reproduced in whole or in part, or stored in a retrieval system, or transmitted in any form or by any means, electronic, mechanical, photocopying, recording, or otherwise, without written permission of the publisher.

Library of Congress Cataloging-in-Publication Data is available on the Library of Congress website

ISBN: 978-1-5157-7460-0 (library binding)
ISBN: 978-1-5157-7470-9 (paperback)
written by Lucia Raatma

Editorial Credits
Christianne Jones, editor; Juliette Peters, designer;
Wanda Winch, media researcher; Laura Manthe, production specialist

Photo Credits
Capstone Studio: Karon Dubke, 11, 15, 17, 21, Juliette Peters, 9; Shutterstock: Angelina Babii, paper texture, Golden Pixels LLC, 7, Mila Supinskaya Glashchenko, 5, MNStudio, 19, Pressmaster, 13, Ronnachai Palas, cover, Samuel Borges Photography, 1, Teguh Mujiono, tree design

Printed in the United States 5329

Table of Contents

Sisters. 4

What Sisters Do 12

Glossary 22

Read More 23

Internet Sites 23

Index. 24

Sisters

Sisters are family. They may have brothers. They may also have sisters.

Mae is a big sister.
She has a sister and
a brother.

Grace and Eli are twins.
They were born on the
same day.

Maria has a brother.

Her brother is a baby.

What Sisters Do

Sky likes to ride her bike.

She rides with her brothers.

Ana's sister likes to read.

She reads to Ana.

Adventure is waiting inside
every MAGIC TREE HOUSE book!

Devon's sister likes to play games. Devon plays with her.

Violet likes to play soccer.

So does her sister.

Sisters play.

They giggle.

They love.

Glossary

brother—a boy who has the same parents as another person

giggle—to laugh in a silly way

sister—a girl who has the same parents as another person

twin—one of two children born at the same time to the same parents

Read More

Robie H. *Who's in My Family?* All About Our Families. Somerville, MA: Candlewick, 2012.

Hunter, Nick. *Finding Out About Your Family History.* Mankato, MN: Heinemann-Raintree, 2015.

Lewis, Clare. *Familes Around the World.* Mankato, MN: Heinemann-Raintree, 2015.

Internet Sites

FactHound offers a safe, fun way to find Internet sites related to this book. All of the sites on FactHound have been researched by our staff.

Here's all you do:
Visit *www.facthound.com*
Type in this code: 9781515774600

Index

babies, 10

biking, 12

brothers, 4, 10, 14

friends, 20

games, 16

giggling, 20

loving, 20

playing, 16, 18, 20

reading, 14

soccer, 18

twins, 8